This Christmas Coloring Book
Belongs To:

____

____

Date: _______ / ____ / ____

Write and Draw to Express Yourself

Date: ___ / ___ / ___

Date: _____ / ____ / _____

Write and Draw to Express Yourself

Date: ___ / ___ / ___

Write and Draw to Express Yourself

Date:

Write and Draw to Express Yourself

Date: _____ / ___ / ______

Date: _____/_____/_____

Write and Draw to Express Yourself

Date: _______ / ___ / ___

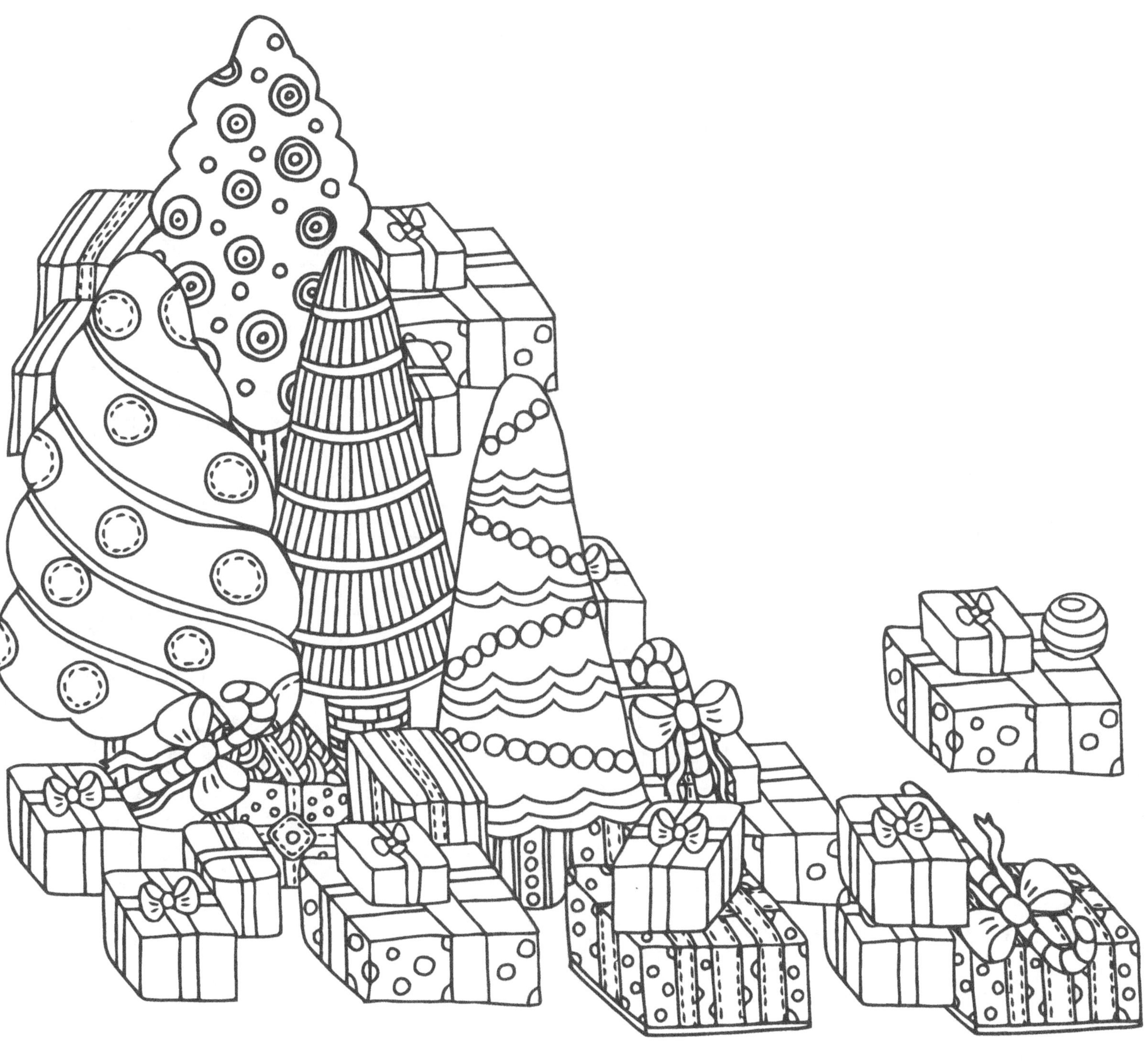

Write and Draw to Express Yourself

Date: _______ / ___ / ___

Write and Draw to Express Yourself

Date: ___ / ___ / ___

Date: _____ / _____ / _____

Write and Draw to Express Yourself

Date:
xmas

Write and Draw to Express Yourself

Date:

Date: _______ / ___ / ___

Date: ___/___/___

Write and Draw to Express Yourself

Date: ___ / ___ / ___

Christmas Time

Write and Draw to Express Yourself

Date: ___/___/___

Write and Draw to Express Yourself

Write and Draw to Express Yourself

Date: ____ / ____ / ____

Write and Draw to Express Yourself

Date: ___ / ___ / ___

Merry
Christmas

Write and Draw to Express Yourself

Date: ___ / ___ / ___

Date: _____ / ___ / _____

Write and Draw to Express Yourself

Date: ___/___/___

Date: ____ / ____ / ____

Write and Draw to Express Yourself

Date: /   /

Date: _______/____/____

Write and Draw to Express Yourself

Date: ___/___/___

Write and Draw to Express Yourself

Date: _____ / ___ / ___

Write and Draw to Express Yourself

Date: ____/____/____

Write and Draw to Express Yourself

Date: ___ / ___ / ___

Write and Draw to Express Yourself

Date: ____ / ____ / ____

Write and Draw to Express Yourself

The
Magic of
Christmas

Write and Draw to Express Yourself

Write and Draw to Express Yourself

Date:

Write and Draw to Express Yourself

Date: _______/_______/_______

Write and Draw to Express Yourself

Date: ___/___/___

Write and Draw to Express Yourself

Date: ___/___/___

Write and Draw to Express Yourself

Date:

Write and Draw to Express Yourself

Date: _______/____/______

Write and Draw to Express Yourself

Date: _______ / ___ / _____

Write and Draw to Express Yourself

peace
&
joy

Date: _____ / ___ / _____

Write and Draw to Express Yourself

Write and Draw to Express Yourself

Date: ___/___/___

Write and Draw to Express Yourself

Date: /   /

Write and Draw to Express Yourself

Write and Draw to Express Yourself

Date:

Date: ____ / ____ / ____

Write and Draw to Express Yourself

Write and Draw to Express Yourself

Write and Draw to Express Yourself

Date: _____ / ____ / _____

www.ingramcontent.com/pod-product-compliance
Lightning Source LLC
Chambersburg PA
CBHW081735250726
48657CB00010B/3271